SOCCER BIOGRAPHIES

SAM KERR

KENNY ABDO

Fly!
An Imprint of Abdo Zoom
abdobooks.com

abdobooks.com

Published by Abdo Zoom, a division of ABDO, P.O. Box 398166, Minneapolis, Minnesota 55439.

Printed in the United States of America, North Mankato, Minnesota.
052025
092025

THIS BOOK CONTAINS RECYCLED MATERIALS

Photo Credits: AP Images, Getty Images, Icon Sportswire, Shutterstock
Production Contributors: Kenny Abdo, Jennie Forsberg, Grace Hansen
Design Contributors: Candice Keimig, Neil Klinepier, Victoria Bates

Library of Congress Control Number: 2024947820

Publisher's Cataloging-in-Publication Data

Names: Abdo, Kenny, author.
Title: Sam Kerr / by Kenny Abdo
Description: Minneapolis, Minnesota : Abdo Zoom, 2026 | Series: Soccer biographies | Includes online resources and index.
Identifiers: ISBN 9781098288877 (lib. bdg.) | ISBN 9781098289577 (ebook) | ISBN 9781098289928 (Read-to-me ebook)
Subjects: LCSH: Women soccer players--Biography--Juvenile literature. | Soccer players--Biography--Juvenile literature. | Professional athletes--Biography-Juvenile literature. | FA Women's Super League--Juvenile literature.
Classification: DDC 796.334092--dc23

TABLE OF CONTENTS

SAM KERR

With her incredible goal-scoring ability and electrifying speed, Sam Kerr is one of the top soccer players in the world!

EARLY YEARS

Samantha Kerr was born in Perth, Australia, in 1993. She grew up in a sports-loving family. Her father was a professional Australian soccer player, inspiring Kerr to reach for greatness.

Kerr started taking soccer seriously at 12 years old. By 15, she joined the **A-League** team Perth Glory, making her **debut** in 2008.

4
NEW ZEALAND
FOOTBALL

GOING PRO

In 2009, Kerr joined the Matildas, the Australian women's national soccer team. By the end of the season, she was honored with the **U20 Footballer of the Year** award. Kerr made her **debut** at the **World Cup** in 2011, helping clinch a second-place finish!

FIFA
20

Kerr joined the National Women's Soccer League (NWSL) in 2013, playing for the Western New York Flash. After the 2014 season, she was traded to Sky Blue FC.

That same year, Kerr returned to Perth Glory. A knee injury knocked her out of the **Olympics**. However, with hard work and recovery, she returned to the field for the 2015 Women's **World Cup** just three months later!

macron
SMARTER
than smoking
macron
PGFC
PGFC

In 2017, Kerr made history by scoring 17 goals in a single season, earning the NWSL Most Valuable Player award. She ended the season as the **AFC** Women's Footballer of the Year.

Kerr became the captain of the Matildas in 2019. Her leadership helped the team collect wins. During the FIFA Women's **World Cup**, Kerr made history by being the first Australian player to score a hat-trick in a World Cup tournament!

In the same year, Kerr joined Chelsea FC Women. Her talent brought the team and all of England many victories. Kerr won her first trophy with Chelsea in a 2–1 victory over Arsenal in the League Cup Final in 2020.

Vitality
Vitality
Vitality
Vitality
Vitality
2020-21 WINNER
FA CUP
CHELSEA

2022-23
WINNER
CHELSEA
FOOTBALL CLUB

In the 2020–21 season, Sam Kerr scored 21 goals for Chelsea, winning the Women's Super League and the **Golden Boot**. At the 2020 Tokyo **Olympics**, she scored the winning goal to send Australia to their first major tournament semi-final.

In 2022, Kerr was given the key to her hometown of Perth to honor her impact on soccer. Sadly, in 2024, Kerr suffered an **ACL** injury that kept her off the field for the rest of the season.

LEGACY

In 2023, Kerr opened her soccer school, Sam Kerr Football (SKF). The school teaches kids about soccer and supports their dreams of going pro. In 2024, SKF partnered with LifeChanger. Together, they help the youth develop social, emotional, and physical strength skills.

CHELSEA
FOOTBALL CLUB

Sam Kerr, Australia's all-time top scorer, is a powerhouse among the world's elite strikers. Kerr proves time and again that she knows how to *net* wins!

AUSTRALIA
20

GLOSSARY

A-League Women – the top-division women's soccer league in Australia.

ACL – short for anterior cruciate ligament, a key ligament in the knee that connects the thighbone to the shinbone.

AFC – short for Asian Football Confederation, the governing body of association football in most countries in Asia.

debut – a first appearance.

Golden Boot – an award given to the league's top goal scorers each season.

Olympic Games – the biggest international athletic event held as separate winter and summer competitions every four years in a different city.

U20 Footballer of the Year – an award that honors players who are 20 years old or younger for their outstanding performances and achievements during the season.

World Cup – an international soccer competition held every four years.

ONLINE RESOURCES

Booklinks
NONFICTION NETWORK
FREE! ONLINE NONFICTION RESOURCES

To learn more about Sam Kerr, please visit **abdobooklinks.com** or scan this QR code. These links are routinely monitored and updated to provide the most current information available.

INDEX